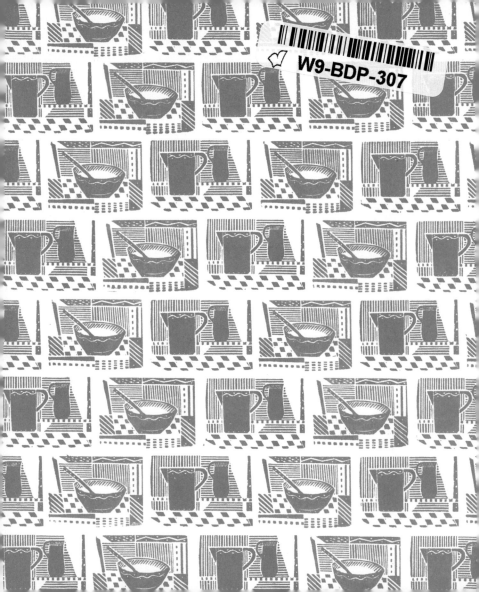

W9-BDP-307

The Country
Cook's Companion

The Country Cook's Companion

Jocasta Innes

Photography by James Merrell

CollinsPublishersSanFrancisco

A Division of HarperCollinsPublishers

First published in USA in 1994 by
Collins Publishers San Francisco
1160 Battery Street
San Francisco CA 94111

First published in l994 by Mitchell Beazley
an imprint of Reed Consumer Books Limited
Michelin House, 81 Fulham Road, London SW3 6RB
and Auckland, Melbourne, Singapore and Toronto

Photography James Merrell
Illustrations Jonathan Gibbs
Recipes Kate Harris

Library of Congress Cataloging-in-Publication Data

Innes, Jocasta.
        The country cook's companion / Jocasta Innes ; photography by
    James Merrell.
            p.   cm. -- (Country companion series)
            Includes index.
            ISBN 0-00-255363-5
            1. Cookery, International. I. Title. II Series.
    TX725.A1I357   1994
    641.59--dc20   93-29787
                                                              CIP

Produced by Mandarin Offset
Printed and bound in China

CONTENTS

In The
Country
Kitchen

INGREDIENTS

Country food, in the main, is unpretentious food, based on what is available locally and in season. That it has become food to be featured on the menus of sophisticated and adventurous restaurants does not detract from its essential simplicity. Dishes include classics such as sausages and polenta, salt cod, thick fish soups, savory country soups halfway to a meal to be eaten with bread and cheese, pork and beans and enormous fruit pies made with wavy rather than perfect crusts.

Squeaky freshness and sizzling immediacy of taste are the qualities we admire and strive for in country cooking, rather than immaculate platefuls where not a whisker of garnish is out of place. Country cooking is about real food made from fresh ingredients, rather than expensive, out-of-season rarities. The rarity that is prized, and appropriate, is of a different sort – freshly gathered vegetables, berries or mushrooms, or newly baked bread.

While true country cooking, wherever in the world it comes from, uses a great variety of such fresh ingredients, it also relies on a store of basic ingredients which must be always to hand if cooking is to be a spontaneous pleasure.

In the days before the refrigerator and

Left: These freshly laid eggs will keep in a cool place for a week, provided that they are transferred to an egg stand which allows them to be stored blunt end up.
Right: Recently caught and gathered mackerel and mussels lie on a slab of cool, hygienic, easily cleaned slate.

freezer many of these foods were either preserved in some way –dried or salted, perhaps, or made into preserves and pickles – or stored in a cool cellar safe from the heat of the kitchen. If you are lucky enough to possess such places

air space fresh eggs have in the blunt end. If eggs have to be stored in the refrigerator, they need to be used quite quickly since eggshells can become moist and porous in cool temperatures, allowing bacteria to penetrate the shell. This

Essential elements in many baking sessions: eggs, whole wheat flour, scales and whisk.

Old-fashioned equipment, still made today, adds to the pleasure of home baking.

today, they can be of almost as much use as the refrigerator or freezer.

Eggs, for instance, one of the cook's most indispensable basic items, will keep well in a cool place for up to a week. They should be kept blunt end up, so the yolk rests on the white rather than in the

point is particularly important with fresh farm eggs, which may have needed washing (which removes their natural protective coating) before being brought indoors.

A cool, draft-free pantry is the best place for keeping most cheeses, too, with the refrigerator being the next best place. For refrigerator storage, cheeses should be wrapped in paper or foil and put in a plastic bag in a temperate part of the refrigerator. Butters should be wrapped for refrigerator storage as they

small quantities in glass jars, but they keep their flavor better when stored in dark-colored jars out of direct light.

Pulses, also basic items in the country kitchen store cupboard, will keep for six to nine months in a cool dry place; kept

Sturdy stoneware bowls may be used both to store and to serve foods and ingredients.

Bowls and baskets pressed into use to store perishables from the kitchen garden.

can pick up odors from stronger-smelling foods. Air-tight storage in a cool place is fine for many of the cook's basic ingredients. Flours, unshelled nuts, oats and other cereals will all keep for up to six months in air-tight containers. Dried herbs and spices may look pretty kept in

for much longer than this, many pulses may become so hard that even long hours of cooking will not soften them.

Many of the ingredients of country cooking do not even need a cupboard for safe storage. Strings of onions and garlic, bunches of herbs, dried sausages

and salamis can be carried on hooks from exposed wood beams which are a frequent feature of country kitchens.

Apples and pears need a cool, dry and airy place for long-term storage. The fruit should be laid out, not touching, on shelves where air can circulate. Both fruits should still have their stalks on and be free of blemishes; apples can be left to ripen on the tree, but pears wanted for storage should be picked before they are ripe. They will be all the more satisfying to use up over the winter months if you know they have come from your own kitchen garden, planted by you with beds of aromatic herbs, unusual salad vegetables and, if you have space, a fruit

tree or two. However, for many of us, the kitchen garden must be a windowsill, roof terrace or balcony: room enough for a satisfying collection of pots brimming with herbs, or even salad stuff. With country cooking, the essentials are good ingredients, in perfect condition, and a cook who can use them well.

Far left: A bunch of herbs just picked from the herb garden rests in a small copper pan.
Left: Home-grown flavorings in a variety of containers, including terra-cotta, pottery, earthenware, wood, china and wicker.
Above: The spices here are, clockwise from top, fenugreek, cinnamon, cumin, paprika and coriander, all in wooden bowls.

COOK'S TOOLS

A few essential tools feature in every cook's *batterie de cuisine*. As well as the classic items like knives and wooden spoons, you should give certain modern gadgets houseroom. Of these, a heavy, robust, well-designed mixer, with the most powerful motor you can afford, is particularly useful.

All cooks must have sharp knives to work with. Start with two or three sizes: 3-inch, 6-inch and 8-inch versions are ideal. Choose knives which have riveted handles and plain, not serrated, blades that you can put an edge on.

You should also have a swivel-bladed peeler for preparing root vegetables or peeling potatoes. And for heavier tasks, go for one of those weighty cleavers stocked by Chinese cookshops. Sharp tools are useless without a good chopping surface to work on. Your chopping board should be heavy, dense (end grain is best) and large.

Choose the best pots and skillets you can afford, ideally copper-bottomed stainless steel skillets with non-heating handles and a lid you can pick up without burning your fingers. As well as a couple of moderate-size skillets, have a 4-quart skillet which can take a colander or round sieve, which will convert the skillet to a steamer, and a shallow, lidded skillet to use for sautéing and braising.

Left: Containers in cool natural materials, including wood, metal, glass and stoneware. Right: Essential cook's tools share a corner of this delightfully decorated kitchen with a varied collection of containers and a shelf of preserves in glass jars.

For stewing or braising the best equipment is a mixture of heavy cast-iron pots which can be used with any type of hob or stove, and that attractive earthenware from France, Spain or Italy. It is inexpensive but must be "seasoned" (heat a layer of oil in it slowly) before use.

The above, plus colanders, sieves (two – one round and one conical, for sauces), wooden spoons and a spatula or two, make up a sensible *batterie de cuisine*.

Another item of importance in the country kitchen is a heavy pestle and

Above: An unusual rack for kitchen utensils.
Left: Everything is for use and to hand in this crowded, but not cluttered kitchen.
Right: Cast aluminum skillets from America.

mortar for pulverizing anything too small or scanty to go through the mixer. There might also be room for one really big pan – a tinned copper preserving skillet, perhaps, or an old-fashioned, enameled metal roasting skillet with a domed lid, often called a Dutch oven.

Not exactly cook's tools, but still essential pieces of kitchen equipment are the many kinds of pottery – earthenware, spongeware, American spatterware, "marbled" ceramics from Provence, Delft and many others – and a collection of containers. Ones for holding food have been made from everything from birch bark to brass, woven straw to hollow gourds. And all are perfectly at home in the country kitchen.

Country
Recipes

STARTERS

Garbure

A hearty, regional French dish. The re
sult will be something between a thick
soup and a liquid stew. The basic ingredients should be navy beans, cabbage
and pork. A selection of vegetables can
be added, chosen according to season.
The French serve this "soup" poured
over slices of bread. The meat can be
chopped into chunks and served in the
soup. Serves 4.

1 cup dried navy beans
1 turnip, diced
2 carrots, diced
2 celery stalks, sliced
1½ cups cubed potatoes
1 pound pork belly or 1 piece boiling ham
1 garlic sausage ring
2-3 cloves garlic, crushed
thyme and / or marjoram
salt and pepper
water or stock
1 cabbage, shredded
1 cup sliced green beans

Soak the navy beans in sufficient cold
water to cover overnight. Drain the
beans, put them in a skillet with fresh
cold water to cover and bring slowly to
a boil. Simmer the beans, covered, for
45-60 minutes.

Add the prepared turnip, carrots, celery
and potatoes, and the meats with the
garlic, herbs, salt and pepper. If you
have any stock, add it to the bean water.
Simmer for 1 hour, skimming off any
scum as it rises in the pan. Now add the
cabbage and green beans. Mix all the ingredients together and cook gently for
another 30-60 minutes.

---

*Right: Garbure (top), Provençal soup with
pistou (middle; for recipe see p. 22) and Leek
and potato soup (bottom; for recipe see p.23)
Previous pages: Oxtail stew (top left; for recipe
see pp. 33-4); Beef casserole Niçoise (bottom
right; for recipe see p. 34); Salt cod cooked in
milk (top right; for recipe see p. 35); and Spicy
sausages with polenta (bottom left; for recipe
see p. 40).*

Provençal Soup with Pistou

This is a simple, solid sort of soup, based on new season's vegetables, as fresh and young as possible, simmered together in plain water with rice to thicken and noodles for substance. The heady aromatic *pistou* brings the dish to life. In Provence, grated cheese is often added for quick protein. There is plenty here to serve 4.

2 tablespoons olive oil
½ cup rice
1 large onion, peeled
½ pound seasonal vegetables: for example, green beans, trimmed and cut in half; fava beans hulled; peas, hulled; zucchini, cut into matchsticks
3-4 new carrots, peeled
4 new potatoes, scrubbed and sliced
½ cup chopped fresh pasta
salt and pepper
Pistou:
3-4 cloves garlic
3-4 sprigs of basil
1 tablespoon pignoli (pine nuts)
1 tablespoon fruity olive oil
½ lemon

An earthenware casserole makes the ideal pot to cook this soup in, stood over a wire mat to diffuse the heat. Otherwise use an enameled cast-iron pot.

Heat the oil gently over low heat and add the rice and onion, turning them in the oil until the onion softens a little. Add all the prepared vegetables and stir around until they are oily and hot, taking care not to let them scorch. Pour over hot water to cover and bring to a boil, then clap on the lid and cook fast for 10 minutes.

Meanwhile, make the *pistou* by simply reducing all the ingredients to a fine paste, either by pounding them together in a mortar or by whirling them in a food blender or food processor. (If you use a blender or processor you may need to add more oil to lubricate the blades.) Set the *pistou* aside.

Drop the pasta into the skillet with the vegetables and cook until *al dente* – about 3-5 minutes. Add salt and pepper to taste. Now stir in the *pistou*, stand for 1-2 minutes to let the aromatics mingle, then serve in shallow bowls. Have freshly grated cheese on the table, to sprinkle over the soup, if you feel like it.
Illustrated on page 21.

Leek and Potato Soup

I feel that savory country soups should be halfway to a meal, eaten with bread and cheese. Tasty and generous, rather than recherché, they all share in common the use of familiar, local foodstuffs.

The quantity below serves 4.

½ stick butter
3 cups cubed potatoes
5 cups sliced leeks
1 lettuce or 2 heads Belgian endive, chopped
a handful of fresh herbs such as parsley, basil and savory
5 cups hot chicken or beef stock
salt and pepper

Melt the butter over a low heat in a deep cast-iron or earthenware pot. Add the chopped prepared vegetables and the chosen herbs and sweat, turning the vegetables frequently until they have softened a little.

Pour on the hot stock, cover the pot and simmer for 1 hour, or until everything is tender and the potatoes are beginning to break up. Add salt and pepper to taste.

Illustrated on page 21.

Iced Sorrel Soup

Sorrel gives a wonderful tang to this summer soup, but young spinach leaves may be used instead if your garden does not run to this vegetable. Serves 4.

1 cucumber, peeled and chopped
1 bunch sorrel leaves, torn into strips
1 clove garlic
4 scallions, finely chopped
4¼ cups chicken stock
⅔ cup light cream
salt and pepper
fresh chives, parsley, chervil or tarragon for garnish

Place the cucumber, sorrel, garlic and scallions in a large pan with the chicken stock and bring to a boil. Simmer until the cucumber and scallions are soft but not mushy.

Let the mixture cool somewhat, then blend until smooth in a food processor or blender. Stir in the cream and mix thoroughly. Add salt and pepper to taste. Serve the soup chilled (ideally, in chilled bowls) with a few finely chopped herbs sprinkled over.

Illustrated on pages 24-5.

Cold Cherry Soup

The rich color ensures that this soup
looks as good as it tastes. Serves 4.

4½ pounds black or morello cherries
3 cloves
½ teaspoon cinnamon
1 cup sugar
half a bottle of red wine
2½ cups water, boiled and cooled
2 tablespoons sour cream as garnish (optional)

With a mallet, crush the cherries and
some of their stones. To get a thicker,
quicker result you could pit the cherries,
then blend in a food processor.

Leave the cherry purée in an earthenware bowl with the spices and the sugar
for a few hours to draw the juices. If you
crushed the cherries you will need to put
them through a coarse sieve to remove
the remaining stones.

Mix in the wine and dilute with water
to taste. Serve chilled, with a dollop of
sour cream, if you like.

———————————

Right: Iced sorrel soup (see p. 23 for recipe)
and Cold cherry soup (far right).

Terrine of Rabbit and Fruit from Alsace

Rabbit has always featured in country cookery, a rabbit for the pot being easy to come by, as a rule. If one large rabbit is unavailable, buy two smaller ones. This is an elegant terrine, good for a buffet or family feast. It should be kept for several days to allow the flavors to develop, so start making it a week ahead of time.

1½ pounds streaky pork, not too fat
a handful of sea salt
3 pounds rabbit – 1 large or 2 small
about 6 tablespoons calvados, marc, or cognac
2 teaspoons salt
1 teaspoon green or black peppercorns
1 carrot
1 small onion
1 stick celery
1 bouquet garni
2-3 tablespoons corn oil
1 egg
1 cup chopped firm plums, preferably green-gages or damsons, pitted
2-3 sprigs of fresh thyme

Left: Terrine of rabbit and fruit from Alsace.

Pork is greatly improved by overnight salting to remove some of its water content. Strip the rind off the meat, then rub a handful of salt – *gros sel* or sea salt is best – well in, all over. Leave in a cool place, or in the refrigerator.

Strip all the meat off the rabbit carcass with a very sharp knife, setting aside some fine pieces whole. Put the meat in a bowl with half the alcohol, the salt and the peppercorns. Cover and marinate in the refrigerator overnight.

The next day, rinse and wipe the pork, cut it into small pieces and add to the rabbit marinade. Leave overnight. Chop the rabbit bones across. Put them in a large skillet with the carrot, onion, celery, bouquet garni and water to cover. Bring to a boil, then lower the heat and simmer until well reduced. (There should be approximately 1 cup.) Strain this stock and set aside.

Pick out the best bits of the rabbit meat and its liver. Heat the oil in a skillet and sauté these pieces of meat lightly. Sprinkle over the remaining alcohol and leave to cool.

Chop the remaining rabbit meat and pork finely together. This can be done easily in a food processor, efficiently with an old-fashioned grinder, and very satis-factorily with a sharp cleaver. Indeed, purists would argue that meats that are chopped by hand with a razor-edged cleaver remain juicier, with more tex-ture. Turn the chopped meat into a large bowl and beat in the egg and re-served stock, then the chopped fruit. Chop the lightly cooked liver, add it to the bowl and mix thoroughly.

Oil a 3-pound terrine and lay 1 sprig of thyme on the base. Half fill with the meat mixture, then lay the lightly cooked rabbit morsels across. Pack in the re-maining meat mixture and finish with another sprig of thyme. Cover with foil and a lid, and place the terrine in a roasting skillet. Add boiling water to a depth of about 1 inch and bake in a pre-heated 350°F oven for 1¼ hours. The terrine is cooked when it starts to shrink away from the sides of the container and feels firm and springy to the fingertip. Leave to cool.

Eat after 4 or 5 days, turned out on a plate and garnished with nasturtium or borage flowers and watercress. A refresh-ing salad of tomatoes and oakleaf lettuce makes a delightful accompaniment for this elegant terrine.

Gazpacho

Although red-hot in color and highly spiced, this Spanish soup is served ice-cold. This quantity feeds 4.

2 slices bread, diced
1 tablespoon oil
1 clove garlic, crushed
¼ cucumber, peeled and diced
½ small onion, peeled and diced
1 pound tomatoes, peeled
1 large onion
2 cloves garlic
1 green bell pepper
½ cucumber, peeled
1 cup tomato juice
cayenne pepper to taste
2-3 tablespoons lemon juice
4-6 tablespoons olive oil

Fry the bread cubes in the oil and garlic. Reserve the resulting croutons, with the diced cucumber, onion and tomato, to serve with the soup.

Purée the tomatoes, onion, garlic, pep-per and cucumber and mix with the tomato juice and cayenne pepper. Add the lemon juice and olive oil a little at a time, tasting frequently to make sure that the soup is neither too sharp nor too oily. Chill well.

Serve in individual bowls with an ice cube floated on top. Fill side dishes with the diced vegetables and croutons.

Add the capers and egg yolk and pound until smooth. Put in the fresh thyme and a trickle of olive oil (the tapenade should not be liquid, just moist enough to spread easily).

Tapenade

Tapenade is a sort of relish, salty and pungent, much eaten in Provence. You can spread it on toast, eat it with cheese, on crackers, even stuff hard-cooked eggs with it. This recipe makes ½ pound.

⅔ cup ripe olives, pitted
⅔ cup green olives, pitted
10 anchovy fillets, drained
1 tablespoon capers, chopped
1 hard-cooked egg yolk
a little fresh thyme
olive oil to moisten

Chop the olives roughly with a knife, then transfer to a mortar. Pound to a paste with a pestle. Pat the anchovy fillets dry with paper towels, then add them to the mortar. Pound until smooth.

Fresh Roe Taramasalata

This is a poor man's taramasalata. The smoked cod's roe traditionally used for this well-known Greek appetizer or dip is deemed a great luxury, and is therefore quite expensive, but the fresh, loose roe of herring are relatively inexpensive. Serves 2-4.

½ pound fresh herring roe
1 tablespoon of butter
small piece of garlic
tiny piece of onion
pinch of salt
dash of lemon juice

Lightly fry the roe in butter in a heavy-bottomed skillet and transfer to a mortar and pestle or a food processor. Mix in the garlic and onion. Season with salt and a dash of lemon juice.

MAIN COURSES

Stuffed Pumpkin

Nowadays, markets sell not only pumpkin in season, but also many of its more arcane relations. Any good dense squash can be stuffed in the same way, but you may need to adjust the quantity of stuffing to suit the size of the squash you have chosen. The quantity here is for an average-size pumpkin and the finished dish should give 6 generous servings.

1 pumpkin
1 heaping tablespoon soft light brown sugar
½ stick butter
1 tablespoon oil
2 onions, finely chopped
1 clove garlic, crushed
½ pound ground lamb or beef
½ cup pignoli (pine nuts)
½ cup slivered almonds
⅓ cup chopped dried or fresh dates
1 teaspoon cinnamon
2 cups cooked rice
salt and pepper

Cut the stalk end off the pumpkin to use as a lid. Scoop out the seeds and the fiber, then spread the brown sugar around the inside with a wooden spoon. Melt the butter in the oil in a large skillet and brown the onions. Add the garlic, then the ground meat, stirring it until it is brown all over.

In a second small skillet lightly toast the pignoli and almonds (use no oil but keep moving the skillet to prevent the nuts from scorching). Add the nuts, dates, cinnamon and rice to the meat. Season with salt and plenty of pepper.

Fill the pumpkin with the savory meat mixture. Fit the stalk end back on top and place the pumpkin on a baking sheet. Bake in a preheated 375°F oven for at least 1 hour or until the pumpkin is soft but not mushy.

Right: Stuffed pumpkin, served in a handmade stoneware dish. Use a ladle to scoop out generous servings of stuffing and pumpkin onto individual plates.

ℛabbit with 𝒫runes

When the harvest has been gathered in, it is time for a celebration meal. Rabbits, bagged or bought from the supermarket, get the luxury treatment with prunes and wine.

2 rabbits
½ cup olive oil
1½ cups red wine
1½ cups dry marsala
1 teaspoon fresh or dried marjoram or thyme
1 cup dried prunes
6 cloves garlic, crushed
ground black pepper

Joint the rabbits, cutting each saddle into 2 pieces. Marinate the meat in 6 tablespoons of the olive oil, the red wine, half the marsala, the thyme and prunes until the prunes are soft. Drain, reserving the marinade and prunes.

Heat the remaining olive oil in a large cast-iron casserole and sauté the garlic and rabbit pieces until the rabbit is browned all over. Pour over the rest of the marsala and turn the rabbit over in

Left: Rabbit with prunes, served with pasta.

it until it has reduced by two-thirds. Pour over the reserved marinade with the prunes. Season with salt, cover, reduce the heat and simmer very gently for 1½-2 hours until the rabbit is very tender. Take the lid off toward the end, if necessary, to reduce the liquid to a rich but plentiful sauce. Pepper it very generously. Serve with a ribbon pasta, such as pappardelle or noodles.

𝒪xtail 𝒮tew

Oxtail makes a rich, thick stew with a good meaty flavor. Plainly cooked vegetables go best with it. Serves 4.

1 medium-sized oxtail, jointed
1 tablespoon all-purpose flour
salt and pepper
¼ stick butter
2 onions, sliced
2 carrots, scraped and diced
1 stalk celery, sliced
1 turnip, peeled and sliced
2 cloves
pinch of mace
juice of ½ lemon

Separate the jointed pieces of oxtail. Wash them, dip them in boiling water for 1 minute, then dry them carefully. Roll the pieces in flour seasoned with salt and pepper.

Melt the butter in a heavy flameproof casserole. When it sizzles, put in the pieces of meat and sliced onions. Turn them over so that the meat browns on all sides. Add the carrots, celery and turnip, with the spices. Pour over enough water to cover the lot. Bring the liquid to a boil, skimming off any scum which rises in the skillet. Reduce the temperature to simmering point, cover the pot with a piece of foil or baking parchment and the lid. Simmer very slowly for 3 hours or longer, if you are not in a hurry. The meat should be very tender.

Taste the stock and add salt and pepper if needed. Should you feel up to it, the appearance of the dish will be improved if you pick out the pieces of meat and put the stock and vegetables through a sieve, returning the thickened stock and meat to the pot for a few minutes to heat up again. However you decide to treat the cooked dish, add the lemon juice just before serving.

Illustrated on pages 18-19.

Beef Casserole Niçoise

This recipe is based on one of those thick, aromatic Mediterranean dishes which smell almost better than they taste. Ideally the casserole should be made with red wine, but thick tomato sauce with a little red wine vinegar added makes an acceptable substitute. Salt pork belly is better than bacon if you can get it. Don't skip the olives unless you really dislike them. They give this dish an unique salty, smoky flavor all their own. This recipe provides 4 generous servings.

2 pounds beef shank
¼ pound salt pork belly or bacon
2 tablespoons corn oil
3 onions, roughly chopped
1 14-oz / 397-g can tomatoes
1 tablespoon red wine vinegar
3 cloves garlic, chopped
3 carrots, thinly sliced
1 bouquet garni
½ teaspoon dried rosemary
salt and pepper
10-12 ripe olives, pitted
tomato paste (optional)
a little boiling water (optional)

34

Cut the beef into thick slices and the pork belly into small strips. Heat the oil in a flameproof casserole. Put the bacon strips in, then add the meat and onions. Turn the meat slices until brown all over. Add the canned tomatoes and wine vinegar with the garlic, carrots, bouquet garni, rosemary, salt and pepper. Heat together until the stew simmers. Alternatively, the above ingredients may be fried in a skillet, then transferred to the casserole.

Transfer the casserole to a preheated moderate oven, 350°F, and cook for 2½ hours. Add the ripe olives, replace the lid and cook for another 30 minutes. If the casserole seems dry you may add a little tomato paste diluted with boiling water. Remove the bouquet garni before serving the casserole.

Illustrated on pages 18-19.

Salt Cod Cooked in Milk

Before the days of the deep freeze, salt fish or meats were essential store cupboard staples, helping country folk through the long winter. Serves 4.

1 pound dried salt cod
2 bay leaves
2-3 tablespoons olive oil
5 large potatoes, peeled and thinly sliced
1 large onion, thinly sliced
1 teaspoon dried oregano
black pepper
1 red or green chili pepper, seeded and chopped
5 cups milk
4 hard-cooked eggs, sliced
12 ripe unpitted olives
a handful of finely chopped parsley
3 cloves garlic, crushed
lemon quarters to serve

Cut the fish into smallish pieces and soak in cold water for 24 hours, renewing the water 2-3 times.

Drain the fish and place in a saucepan with cold water to cover. Add the bay leaves and bring to a simmer, but do not let the water boil or the cod will toughen. Simmer for 5 minutes, then take off the heat and let stand for 30 minutes.

Drain the fish, removing the gray skin and bones, and flake coarsely. Cover the base of a wide flameproof earthenware dish with oil, then fill with layers of potatoes, sliced onion and flaked fish, sprinkling oregano and black pepper and chili as you go. Pour over milk to just cover, then bake or simmer on top of the stove until the potatoes are tender and the milk has been absorbed.

Decorate the dish with sliced egg and ripe olives and add a sprinkling of parsley and garlic.

Illustrated on pages 18-19.

Date and Mussel Risotto

Arborio rice is traditionally used for Italian risottos, although American long-grain rice makes a tasty, if less authentic substitute. Serves 4.

24 mussels, scrubbed and debearded
½ bottle white wine
½ stick butter
2 tablespoons oil
3 cloves garlic, crushed
2 leeks, sliced
2 cups arborio rice
½ teaspoon powdered saffron, or to taste
⅔ cup halved fresh or preserved dates, pitted
salt and pepper
brown sugar to taste

Put the mussels into a heavy saucepan over a moderate heat and add the white wine. Cover and "sweat" the mussels for 5-8 minutes until they open. Using a slotted spoon, transfer the mussels to a bowl. Discard any that are not open. Set the liquid aside.

Melt half the butter in the oil in a wide skillet and heat the crushed garlic and leeks for 1-2 minutes. Stir in the rice. When the rice turns translucent start to tip in some of the reserved liquid from the mussels. When all the juice is absorbed, continue with water until the rice is almost ready. Now add the saffron, dissolved in a little boiling water. Meanwhile, discard a few mussel shells, though it's pretty to keep some.

In a second skillet melt the remaining butter and add the dates. Add the slimmed-down heap of mussels. (You can melt a teaspoon of brown sugar in now if you are using fresh dates and would like the dish exotically sweet; preserved dates will be sweet enough.) When the dates are warmed through and buttery, stir them into the risotto. Add water cautiously until the rice is cooked – though still with a bite. Taste, season with pepper and serve.

Above:Date and mussel risotto looks attractive served on a brightly painted Italian plate.

Potato Pie

Serve this pie hot, or pack it cold for eating at a picnic. Serves 12.

Yeast dough:
¼ teaspoon sugar
1¼ cups tepid water
1 packet active dry yeast
4 cups all-purpose flour
pinch of salt
¾ stick butter, softened
1 egg
Filling:
1 pound ground pork
handful of spinach, sorrel or chard, chopped
handful of parsley, finely chopped
2-3 cloves garlic, crushed
3 shallots or 4-5 scallions, minced
salt and pepper
a sprinkling of ground mace or grated nutmeg
6 cups sliced potatoes

Dissolve the sugar in half the tepid water. Add the yeast, stir and leave for 10 minutes until frothy. Warm the flour and salt slightly in a large bowl. Cut in the butter. Make a well in the flour, then stir in the yeast liquid with the beaten egg, adding enough of the remaining water to make a soft dough. Knead until smooth and elastic then return the dough to a clean bowl, cover and leave to rise in a warm place for 2 hours.

Preheat the oven to 425°F. Make the meat and herb pie filling. Mix the minced pork with the spinach, sorrel or chard. Add the parsley, garlic, shallots or scallions and seasonings.

On a floured board, roll out three-quarters of the dough thinly and line a 12-inch pie dish, bringing the yeast dough up the sides and leaving a lip all around. Fill the pie with alternate layers of potato slices and pork mixture, finishing with the pork. Roll out the remaining dough to fit the top of the pie. Fit in place, and damp and seal the edges. Cut a hole in the middle of the crust for steam to escape.

Bake the pie for 20 minutes to get the yeast dough off to a good start, then lower the heat to 350°F and bake for 1 hour more, capping the pie with foil toward the end of this time, to stop the crust overbrowning.

Right: Potato pie, cooked in a simple white baking dish.

Spicy Sausages with Polenta

Polenta is one of those comforting preparations, like mashed potato, which act as complement and blotting paper to highly seasoned or spiced foods, while contributing a soothing texture and taste of their own. The polenta is prepared ahead of time, so that it has time to get completely cold and quite dense. When cold, it is cut into squares and crisped in the oven, then served with the sausages (which should be the best pure meat country sausages around), arranged on top. The rich sauce is usually served separately.

Serves 4-6.

8-12 good-size all-meat sausage links, with herbs or spices
4 tablespoons red wine or water, or a mixture of the two
Polenta:
4 cups salted water
3 cups fine-grain cornmeal
¼ stick butter
1 cup shredded hard cheese such as Parmesan, Pecorino, Cheddar, or a mixture of two or three kinds

Sauce:
2-3 tablespoons corn or olive oil
1 large onion, chopped
1 carrot, chopped
1 celery stalk, chopped
2 pounds tomatoes, or canned equivalent
1 small bunch of parsley, stalks tied
1 fat clove garlic, crushed
¾ ounce dried mushrooms, soaked in warm water
½ cup red wine
salt and pepper

Polenta used for baking needs to be made far enough ahead to cool. Make it the night before or early in the morning. Bring the salted water to a rapid boil in a heavy pot, preferably enameled cast-iron, then tip the cornmeal in a steady stream into the pot, stirring constantly. After a minute or two it will thicken dramatically. Stirring will become harder, even laborious. Italians claim that they stand stirring for half an hour for perfect polenta, but I find that reducing the heat to a whisper and giving the mixture an occasional vigorous stir with a wooden spoon breaks up any threatening lumps and concentrates the texture. Give it about 40 minutes. Then spoon out onto an oiled board, marble slab or large platter. Smooth over and allow to cool.

To bake the polenta, cut into diamonds or squares. Lay these overlapping one another in an ovenproof dish, dot with the butter and dredge with the shredded cheese. Bake at 400°F for 30-40 minutes until the polenta is crisp and golden-brown on top.

Meanwhile, cook the sausage links at the bottom of the oven. Prick the skins, lay them in a roasting pan, add the red wine or water, cover with foil and bake for 30 minutes, turning now and then.

While the sausages are cooking, prepare the sauce. Heat the oil in a skillet and soften the onion, carrot and celery. Add the tomatoes, parsley and garlic. Drain the mushrooms, adding their soaking water to the pan. Chop the mushrooms and add them too. Bring to a fairly fast boil and cook covered until the vegetables soften. Add the red wine, reduce the heat and simmer until thickened and tasty. Add salt and pepper to taste. For the last 10 minutes, if you wish, the sausages can be added to the sauce to allow flavors to blend, or the sauce can be served separately.

Illustrated on pages 18-19.

Pork and Beans

Also called Boston Baked Beans, this is an American classic. Serves 4.

2 cups dried navy beans soaked overnight in water
2 tablespoons molasses
a dash of Worcestershire sauce
2½ teaspoons dry mustard
2½ teaspoons soft light brown sugar
salt and pepper
½ pound streaky pork (salt or otherwise), derinded and cut into chunks
1 large onion, sliced

Cook the beans for 1½-2 hours in the water they were soaked in. Strain, reserving the water in a clean skillet. Put the beans in a casserole and set aside.

Heat the bean water and stir in the molasses, Worcestershire sauce, mustard, sugar, salt and pepper. Add the pork and onion to the beans, then pour over the bean water. If necessary, add hot water to come just over the top of the beans.

Cover and bake in a preheated 350°F oven for about 1 hour or until the beans are soft. If the beans seem to be getting dry, add more hot water.

Chick Peas Catalan

This adaptation of a Catalan dish serves
4 people. Some delicatessens stock
chorizos, but any highly spiced
European-style boiling sausage could
be substituted.

2 cups chick peas, soaked in water for 12
hours, rinsed and drained
1 large onion, roughly chopped
1 carrot, scraped and sliced
1 stalk celery, sliced
1 ham bone with trimmings
1 bouquet garni
3 tablespoons olive oil
1 chorizo or other spiced sausage
2½ cups homemade tomato sauce or
1 5-ounce can tomato purée
1 clove garlic, crushed
2 tablespoons chopped parsley
salt and pepper

Put the chick peas in plenty of fresh
water in a large skillet with the onion,
carrot and celery. Push the ham bone
down among the chick peas, together

with the bouquet garni. Add 2 tablespoons of the oil to the cooking water.

Bring the contents of the skillet slowly
to a boil, skimming if necessary, and boil
steadily over lowest heat for 2 hours or
until the chick peas are tender. Add the
sausage and cook for a further 2-3 hours.

Strain the stock into a bowl, remove
the bouquet garni and transfer the chick
peas, vegetables and bacon to a flameproof casserole.

If you are using tomato sauce, dilute it
with enough of the cooking liquid to
cover the peas. If you are using tomato
paste, mix the contents of the can with
the stock. Pour the liquid over the peas,
mixing well. Continue cooking, covered,
on top of the stove over a low heat for
another 1-2 hours. Alternatively, bake
the dish, covered, in a preheated oven at
325°F for about the same length of time.
If the dish seems to be getting too dry,
add any remaining stock from the peas
or a little boiling water. About 15 minutes before serving, stir in the garlic,
parsley and remaining olive oil. Add salt
and pepper to taste and remove the bouquet garni. The dish should be served
with the sausage cut into chunks and the
ham removed from the bone.

Left: Chick peas Catalan, cooked in an Aga.

Fettucine with Broccoli and Anchovy

This recipe seems almost too primitive to be interesting, so simple is its method: chopped broccoli is heated through with anchovies melted into a *salsa verde* mixture of herbs and garlic, the whole lot stirred into a heap of fine noodles. Quick, satisfying and delicious, it is an excellent way to make one or two bundles of broccoli feed 4 or so people in style. You could serve a salad beforehand, but the pasta should be eaten solo.

1 pound broccoli
salt and plenty of freshly ground black pepper
4 cups freshly-made fettucine
6 tablespoons extra-virgin olive oil
8 canned anchovy fillets plus some of
the oil from the can
4-6 cloves garlic, finely chopped
a generous handful of parsley
and/or basil, finely chopped

It is best to cook the broccoli stems ahead of the florets, otherwise by the time the stems are *al dente* the tops will be a mush. Cut off the stems just below the heads, and throw into a skillet of boiling salted water. After 3 minutes add the florets, and cook for another 2-3 minutes. The broccoli should be just crisp and green, as it will get more cooking during the final assembly stage. Drain.

Meanwhile, drop the fettucine into a large skillet of boiling salted water, stirring briefly to loosen the ribbons of pasta. Turn the heat down slightly and cook for 2-3 minutes until *al dente*. Drain and refresh under cold running water. Drain thoroughly again.

When cold, cut the broccoli into smallish pieces – not a mush nor big chunks, but somewhere in between. Set aside.

In a large flameproof dish on a low flame, first heat the olive oil, then add the chopped anchovy fillets and a little of their oil. When the anchovies disintegrate, add the chopped garlic and herbs. Heat for 1 minute over gentle heat, stirring well to prevent the garlic from burning. Add the broccoli, forking it around in the anchovy mixture until hot. Finally, add the fettucine, forking it around briskly to coat and loosen.

Right: Fettucine with broccoli and anchovy.

SALADS AND VEGETABLES

Bean and Cucumber Salad

Early in the season, when fava beans are small and very tender, they are good eaten lightly blanched as a salad. The quantities for this salad are enough to serve 2-4.

1 pound fava beans, hulled
2 teaspoons chopped fresh herbs
1 cucumber, finely diced
Dressing:
1 egg, hard-cooked
2-3 tablespoons light cream

Bring a skillet of water to a boil, add the hulled beans and cook them for 1 minute. Drain the beans into a colander, refresh under cold running water and drain again.

Mix the beans, the chosen herbs and diced cucumber in a bowl.

To make the dressing, separate the egg yolk and white. Chop the white, pound the yolk and mix the two together. Moisten with the cream.

Pour the dressing over the salad just before you want to serve it.

A few shrimps could be added to turn this simple salad into a light meal, augmented with fresh whole wheat bread or a French stick.

Left: Green beans Provençale (left; see p. 49 for recipe) and Tuscan bread and tomato salad (right; see p. 49 for recipe).
Right: Warm pepper salad (left; see p. 48 for recipe) and Bean and cucumber salad (top; recipe is on this page).

Warm Pepper Salad

Now that bell peppers, in their gorgeous motley of green, scarlet and gold, are available all year around, you can make this salad as often as you like. Dress it copiously, and let it stand for five minutes before serving with crusty bread to mop up the delicious juices.

1 large bell pepper per person
4 tablespoons olive oil
2 anchovy fillets per pepper
2-3 fat cloves garlic, crushed
1-2 tablespoons capers, drained and chopped
salt and pepper

Broil the peppers. The easiest way to do this, I find, is to sit them on a gas ring, one at a time, turning them as they blacken. More elegant is to skewer them on a fork and turn them in the flame, which can also be a wood fire or barbecue. If these methods are not possible, cut the peppers in half and layer them in a broiler skillet lined with foil. Broil them until the skin chars all over and becomes flaky. Then carefully peel away the blackened outer skin, leaving the partly-cooked pepper with a sweet intensity of flavor and a limp, juicy texture.

As each pepper cooks, transfer it to a plastic bag to steam gently (this makes the skin easier to remove) while you prepare the lusty Sicilian dressing.

For the dressing, gently heat the olive oil in a small skillet and mash in the anchovies, stirring until they dissolve into the oil. Add the crushed garlic and the chopped capers with salt and pepper to taste. Stir briefly then remove from the heat but keep warm.

Next, take a pepper, and with a blunt knife scrape off as much charred outer skin as you can. Halve the pepper and remove the seeds, membranes and stalk. To loosen any last clinging black shreds, run the pepper under a cold tap, or dip it into cold water, and use your fingernails. A little charred skin left behind will not wreck the flavour, but it will mar the look of the dish.

As each pepper is dealt with, cut it lengthwise into thick strips and lay these in a dish with the dressing, turning to coat them. Repeat this process until you have filled the dish – a flat, oval or round pottery dish is becoming – and then serve the salad.

Illustrated on page 47.

Tuscan Bread and Tomato Salad

Although this Tuscan salad made with stale bread and tomatoes is very simple to make, this does not prevent it appearing on menus of smart restaurants specializing in rustic food. Eat as an appetizer, or with something light like an omelet, sliced salami or prosciutto, or broiled fish. There is plenty here for 4.

6 or more chunks of hard, stale bread
6 ripe, juicy tomatoes, peeled and roughly chopped
1 large onion, or 1 bunch of scallions, peeled and chopped quite small, but with some green left on
½ cucumber, part-peeled and diced
1 large sprig of basil and/or parsley, finely chopped
1 clove garlic, crushed
3 tablespoons fruity olive oil
salt and pepper
2 tablespoons red wine vinegar

Soak the bread in cold water for 15 minutes. Squeeze out as much water as possible, then crumble into a large bowl.

Add the chopped vegetables, herbs, garlic, olive oil, salt and pepper and fork through the mix. Chill the salad for 1-2 hours, adding vinegar to taste and a sprinkle more herbs just before serving. *Illustrated on page 46.*

Green Beans Provençale

To serve beans cooked in this way cold, use olive oil instead of butter and squeeze lemon juice over them. This quantity serves 4.

1 pound snap beans or haricots verts, trimmed
salt
1 tablespoon butter
1 clove garlic, peeled but left whole
2 anchovies, pounded until smooth

Put the beans into a skillet of boiling salted water and cook until tender. Drain. Melt the butter with the garlic in a skillet over gentle heat. Add the beans and stir until they have absorbed the butter. Stir in the anchovies and heat through. Remove the garlic clove before serving. *Illustrated on page 46.*

Dandelion Salad

Young dandelion leaves make a tasty salad, either mixed with other greens or on their own. If there are dandelions in your garden, make them more tender by laying a tile over the plant. With wild ones, use the youngest leaves only.

dandelion leaves
assortment of salad greens
3-4 bacon slices, cut in squares
1 tablespoon red wine vinegar

Below: Dandelion salad, with a tart dressing.
Right: West Coast salad, from California.

Wash and dry the dandelion leaves and other greens and set aside, whole, in a serving dish. To make the dressing, put the bacon squares into a skillet over a moderate heat, until the fat has melted a bit and the bacon is crisp. Quickly stir the vinegar into the fat, and pour the whole lot over the salad.

West Coast Salad

A salad from Richard Irving of the Ivy Restaurant, Los Angeles. Serves 4.

2 ears of corn
1 pound zucchini
1 pound mushrooms
1 bunch spring onions
1 pound shrimp in shells
1 head radicchio, shredded
1 head oakleaf lettuce, shredded
1 cucumber, roughly chopped
2 avocados, peeled and chopped
4 tomatoes, peeled and chopped
Vinaigrette:
2 tablespoons olive oil
1 tablespoon red wine vinegar
1 teaspoon ground chili powder

Barbecue or charcoal grill the whole corn, zucchini, mushrooms, scallions and shrimp. Meanwhile, mix the radicchio, lettuce, cucumber, avocado and tomato together and toss them into the spicy vinaigrette. Strip the grilled corn from its cob and add it to the cold ingredients, along with the other grilled vegetables, chopped, and the shrimp. Serve with wedges of lime and lemon.

Smoked Mackerel Salad

Smoked tuna may be substituted for mackerel in this salad. Serves 4.

1 smoked mackerel
1 pound new potatoes
1 onion, finely chopped
1 small radicchio or oakleaf lettuce, shredded
Dressing:
6 tablespoons olive or hazelnut oil
2 tablespoons white wine vinegar
¼ teaspoon dry mustard
salt and pepper

Bone and skin the mackerel and cut into even slices. Scrub the potatoes and boil them for 15-20 minutes or until tender. Make the dressing by shaking all the ingredients together in a screw-top jar.

When the potatoes are ready, cut them up roughly and return them to the warm skillet – turn the heat up high and quickly throw in the onion, the radicchio or lettuce and the dressing. After a few seconds put the salad into a bowl and add the mackerel pieces. Serve immediately.

Right: The mackerel salad with radicchio.

BAKING

Barm Brack

This delicious sweet and fruity bread is a traditional Celtic recipe.

2 tablespoons soft light brown sugar
1¼ cups lukewarm milk
1 package active dry yeast
4 cups all-purpose or bread flour
⅔ cup golden raisins
½ cup dried currants
2 tablespoons candied peel
½ stick butter or margarine
a pinch of allspice
a pinch of salt
1 egg, beaten
1 tablespoon clear honey to glaze

Dissolve 1 teaspoon of the sugar in half the milk. Add the yeast, stir and leave for 10 minutes until frothy. Warm the flour slightly in one bowl and the dried fruit and peel in another. Rub the fat into the flour, then stir in the fruit, peel, spice, remaining sugar and salt and mix well.

Make a well in the flour, add the yeast mixture and the egg, then as much of the remaining warm milk as is needed to make a soft dough. Knead until smooth and elastic, then return the dough to the clean bowl, cover and leave to rise in a warm place for 2 hours.

Turn out the risen dough onto a floured board and knead for 5 minutes. Put into a greased, warmed 7-cup loaf skillet and place in an oiled plastic bag to rise for 30 minutes.

Bake the Barm brack in a preheated 400°F oven for 10 minutes. Lower the heat to 325°F and cook for a further 30-45 minutes, or until the bread is firm and has shrunk away slightly from the sides of the tin.

Invert the bread onto a cooling rack. While it is still hot, brush the top with the honey to glaze. Barm brack is traditionally eaten cold.

Right: Soda bread (left; for recipe see p. 56), Barm brack (top; recipe above), Buttermilk biscuits (bottom; for recipe see p. 56).

Buttermilk Biscuits

If buttermilk is not available, you should substitute sour milk (thickened but not separated). Makes 12.

2 cups all-purpose flour
1 teaspoon baking powder
pinch of salt
¼ stick butter or margarine
¼ teaspoon baking soda
⅔ cup buttermilk

Preheat the oven to 400°F. Sift the flour, baking powder and salt into a mixing bowl. Cut in the butter and rub it in until the mixture resembles fine crumbs. Dissolve the soda in the buttermilk and stir into the dry ingredients until the dough is smooth and leaves the bowl's sides clean.

On a floured board, roll the dough out to a thickness of about ¾ inch. Stamp out into about 12 rounds. Lay these on a greased baking sheet.

Bake for 10 minutes then reduce the oven temperature to 350°F and cook for another 5-10 minutes, or until the biscuits are golden.

Illustrated on page 55.

Soda Bread

The traditional Irish bread, made without yeast. A handful of currants or golden raisins added to the dough make it into a nice tea bread which can be eaten hot with butter. The bread should be made with buttermilk, but ordinary milk which has gone sour (thickened but not separated) may be substituted.

4 cups all-purpose flour
1 teaspoon salt
1 teaspoon baking soda
1 teaspoon sugar (optional)
buttermilk

Sift the dry ingredients into a large bowl. Make a well in the middle and gradually add the buttermilk, little by little, stirring in the flour at the same time, until you have a soft dough and the bowl is fairly clean. Preheat the oven to 425°F.

Transfer the dough to a floured board and knead lightly then pat out into a round about 1¼ inches thick.

Lay the dough round on a lightly greased baking sheet and make a cross-shaped cut in the middle. Bake for about 35 minutes. Remove the bread from the baking sheet and tap the bottom to make sure that it is cooked through – it should sound hollow. Set it to cool or eat warm. *Illustrated on page 55.*

Dried Apricot Jam

This jam can be made all-year-around as dried apricots have no season. The grapefruit supplies acid – two lemons can be substituted. These ingredients make about 3 pounds.

¾ pound dried apricots
7½ cups boiling water
4 cups sugar
juice of 1 large grapefruit or 2 lemons
2-3 tablespoons slivered almonds

Wash the apricots, put them in a large bowl and pour over the boiling water. Leave for 1-3 days, until the apricots are swollen and soft.

Turn the apricots and soaking liquid into a skillet and simmer until tender. Add the sugar, grapefruit or lemon juice and almonds. Bring to a boil and boil until the jam reaches the setting point.

Test after 10 minutes, by dropping some on a saucer and setting it in a cool place for 1-2 minutes. The jam should wrinkle at the edges, and when you run a finger through the center, it should stay in two sections. Pot, seal and cover.

Lemon Cheese

This recipe makes about 1½ pounds and is very good indeed.

½ pound sugar cubes
2 large lemons
¾ stick butter
3 eggs, beaten

Rub the sugar cubes over the lemons so that they absorb the flavored oil from the skin. Put the sugar cubes in the top of a double boiler. Add the butter. Squeeze the juice from the lemons and add to the skillet with the beaten eggs.

Set the skillet over barely simmering water and cook, stirring constantly, until the mixture thickens. Pour into jars. When the lemon cheese is cold, store it in the refrigerator.

Cherry Tart

One of the most beautiful-looking open fruit tarts. Make it when cherries are at their ripest, using the dark, sweet kind, or you could use canned cherries.

In both cases, the stones should be removed. This is a tedious job, but it greatly improves the tart. Serves 6.

Below: Cherry tart (left) and Spiced apple tart (right; recipe opposite).

2-2¼ pounds dark cherries, pitted
½ cup sugar
3 tablespoons red currant jelly
1 tablespoon water
Pie dough:
1 cup all-purpose flour plus extra for rolling
¼ teaspoon salt
½ stick margarine

Make the pie dough: sift the flour and salt into a bowl. Cut, then rub in the fat. Add cold water to make a stiff dough.

Roll out the dough on a floured surface and line an 8-inch flan ring set on a baking sheet.

Arrange the pitted cherries close together on the dough. Sprinkle with the sugar. Bake for 30-40 minutes in a preheated 400°F oven.

When the tart has cooled a little, melt the currant jelly in a pan with the water, and pour over the top of the cherries to glaze them attractively.

Spiced Apple Tart

This tart has a batter base, not dough, and gives 4-6 generous servings.

5 biggish cooking or firm eating apples
juice of 1 lemon
Batter:
10 tablespoons self-raising flour
pinch of salt
1 teaspoon ground cinnamon (more if you like)
⅓ cup superfine sugar
½ cup milk
1 drop of vanilla extract
2 eggs
4 tablespoons corn oil

Topping:
sugar for dusting
½ stick butter
½ cup broken walnuts

Peel the apples. Slice them into a bowl and pour lemon juice over them to stop them browning. Grease a medium-sized tart dish or cake skillet and set aside. Preheat the oven to 400-425°F.

Make a batter with the flour, salt, cinnamon, sugar, milk, vanilla extract, eggs and oil, something which can be done very quickly in a food processor or blender. Alternatively, mix the dry ingredients together in a bowl, make a well in the middle and add the liquids. Beat well, gradually incorporating the flour until a smooth batter is formed.

Pour the batter into the greased tart dish. Arrange the slices of apple on top of the batter – in a haphazard way or lined up with patisserie smartness, just as you like.

Scatter a little more sugar, small lumps of butter and the broken walnuts all over the flan and bake it for 30-45 minutes, until it has puffed up and become golden in color. The tart can be served hot for dessert or cold for a snack.

Dur Mou

This old French family recipe starts with a basic chocolate mousse mixture made with lots of eggs and ends up with something between a soufflé and a squidgy cake. You sandwich a layer of the chocolate mousse mixture between two layers of the *dur mou* for a wickedly rich result – so rich that this recipe may give up to 8 servings.

11 oz dark German chocolate
2 sticks sweet butter
1 cup superfine sugar
9 egg yolks
pinch of salt
5 egg whites

Preheat the oven to 300°F. Melt the chocolate with the butter in the top of a double boiler set over simmering water. Beat the sugar with the egg yolks until smooth. Mix this with the chocolate away from the heat, adding it gradually. Beat the egg whites in a clean bowl with

a tiny pinch of salt until stiff. Using a metal spoon, fold the egg whites into the chocolate mixture gently but thoroughly.

Have prepared a pair of 7 ¼-inch skillets oiled or lined with non-stick baking parchment. Divide approximately two-thirds of the batter between the two skillets, place into the oven and bake for 1 hour. Reserve the rest of the cake batter/mousse and place in the refrigerator.

Once the cakes are baked, cool them then chill them in the skillets. Take the reserved mousse from the refrigerator and spoon it carefully over one of the cakes (both now removed from their skillets). Put the other cake on top, to sandwich the two halves together.

Left: A generous slice of Dur mou ready for eating, and (right) a whole cake.

Strawberry Cream

Crushed strawberries have twice as much flavor as the whole fruit, which seem to get ruddier and more insipid every year. This recipe brings out whatever taste they have. Serves 2-3.

1½ cups quartered ripe strawberries
1 tablespoon sugar
juice of ½ lemon
1 envelope unflavored gelatin
2 tablespoons warm water
2 tablespoons warm milk
1¼ cups heavy cream
almond oil for greasing (optional)

Mash the strawberries, discarding any moldy or badly bruised ones and push them through a fine sieve into a bowl. (A plastic sieve will do, but not metal.) Stir in the sugar and lemon juice.

Sprinkle the gelatin onto the warm water in a small bowl and set aside until spongy. Add the warm milk. Set the bowl over hot water and stir the gelatin until it dissolves. Strain it onto the strawberry purée. Whip the cream and stir it into the strawberry mixture. Transfer the strawberry cream to a bowl or mold and either keep in the refrigerator or in a cool place until needed. If you want to turn the cream out, smear the mold very thinly with flavorless oil first. Almond oil is the correct thing, but vegetable (not olive) oil does just as well.

Junket and Cream

Junket is simple and unpretentious. Serve it with thick cream for a real treat. Serves 4.

2 cups whole milk
2-3 tablespoons sugar
1 teaspoon prepared rennet
⅔ cup heavy cream
grated nutmeg or ground cinnamon

Heat the milk in a saucepan over low heat until just tepid. Add sugar to taste, stirring well. Pour into a flat dish, stir in the rennet and let set. Pour over the cream and sprinkle with spice to serve.

Right: Strawberry cream in an antique mold and Junket and cream in heart-shaped dishes.

Index

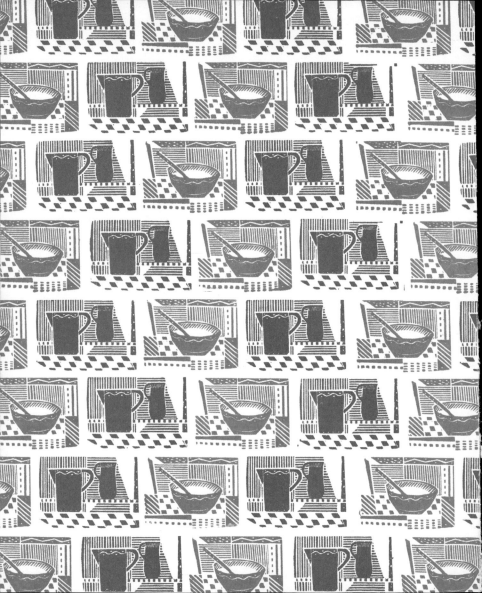